Let Love Lead

Reclaiming the Power of Black Love

By Professor Lewis Miles

and

Dr. Charmaine Marie, Ed.D.

Published by: Real LOVE Publications

Let Love Lead

Reclaiming the Power of Black Love

By Professor Lewis Miles

and

Dr. Charmaine Marie

Copyright © 2025 by: Real LOVE Publications.

All rights reserved

No part of this publication may be reproduced, stored in a retrieval system or transmitted in any way by any means, electronic, mechanical, photocopy, recording or otherwise without the prior permission of the author except as provided by USA copyright law.

This book is a work of nonfiction. Descriptions, entities, and incidents included in the story are exclusively products of the author's imagination. Any resemblance to events, and entities is entirely coincidental.

ISBN#: 978-1-7377075-9-2

Printed in the United States of America

Thank you for taking the time to read,

Let Love Lead

Reclaiming the Power of Black Love

We hope you enjoy the book.

Please do a book review on Amazon.com

to let us know what you think.

1 Corinthians 13:4-7 NIV

Love is patient, love is kind. It does not envy, it does not boast, it is not proud. It does not dishonor others, it is not self-seeking, it is not easily angered, it keeps no record of wrongs. Love does not delight in evil but rejoices with the truth. It always protects, always trusts, always hopes, always perseveres.

Dear Reader,

Every story worth telling must, at some point, pass through the heart. This book is a journey through the heart, led by two lifelong friends, Dr. Charmaine Marie and Professor Lewis Miles, who have known love, lost trust, wrestled with pain, and now stand in the soft, sacred space where healing begins.

Let us be clear from the very start: We are not a couple. We are not married. We are two individuals, a Black woman and a Black man, who have shared a 30+ year friendship built on honesty, respect, and real conversations.

This book is a reflection of those conversations. Born from our personal experiences, our individual truths, and our mutual desire to see our people whole again, we came together to speak to the fractures we've seen in love, especially Black love, and to explore the ways we can mend them.

We don't pretend to have all the answers. What we do have is perspective, wisdom gained through lived experience, and the courage to say what often goes unsaid. These pages offer us both the rare gift of time and space to examine what love looks like in our lives, its glory, its gaps, and its growing pains. You'll witness us reflecting on the relationships that shaped us, the ones that gave us hope, and the ones that left us holding pieces we had to put back together.

But this isn't just about looking back, it's about building forward. We challenge each other, we respond to each other, and we hold space for each other, with no script and no pretense. We believe that real healing happens when men and women listen to one another, not to win, but to understand.

This is a book built on that principle: Truth + Grace = Transformation. So, as you read, don't just look through the window into our lives, hold up the mirror to your own. Reflect. Reconsider. Reconnect. Ask yourself:

- What do I need to heal from?
- Who have I become because of the love I've known, or the pain I've carried?
- Am I willing to listen, truly listen, with an open heart and a teachable spirit?

These chapters are an invitation to that kind of listening, not just with your ears, but with your whole heart. Let this be your soft turning point. Let this be the breath between the battles. Let this be the bridge over what's been broken. Let this be your new beginning wrapped in old wisdom.

    We're not here to place blame. We're here to invite becoming! Becoming better. Becoming healed. Becoming ready. Welcome to the moment when healing begins. Let the conversations shape you. Let the honesty stretch you. And let love, real love, lead the way.

Chapter 1

Unseen, Yet Unshakable:

How I Feel About The Black Woman

Professor Lewis Miles

The relationship between Black men and Black women is at a crossroads. Over time, deep-seated frustrations, unspoken expectations, and societal shifts have reshaped how we see and treat one another. Many Black women feel exhausted by the weight of disappointment and lack of support from Black men. At the same time, many Black men feel abandoned, believing that as Black women rise in independence and success, they are leaving them behind rather than uplifting them.

The struggle is real. Black women want to be valued, appreciated, and respected for the sacrifices they have made to achieve their success. Yet, instead of receiving admiration, some feel resentment from the very men they long to build with. On the other hand, Black men often feel like their role as providers and leaders has been stripped away. The shifting dynamics in relationships make them question whether they still have a place, as the traditional expectations of a man's leadership seem to be diminishing.

This divide has left many Black relationships fractured, with crucial conversations left unspoken. As a result, a growing disconnect is affecting not just individuals but future generations. The absence of understanding between Black men and women has rippled into the lives of our sons and daughters, influencing their views on love, respect, and partnership.

We are at a turning point where our relationships are becoming increasingly fragile. The question is: What can we do to heal? How do we address the pain and frustrations that have built up over time? How can we rebuild trust, respect, and unity in Black relationships?

This is an honest reflection on the current state of Black relationships, laying the foundation for deeper conversations that need to be had. Let's address the issues, understand the root causes, and, most importantly, find a way forward together.

Unseen, Yet Unshakable:
How I Feel About The Black Man

Dr. Charmaine Marie

I love the Black man. I am intrigued by him. I admire him. I respect him. He comes in all shapes, sizes, and shades, and each one carries a unique beauty that captivates me. I love the different textures of his hair, the strength in his presence, the depth of his intelligence. The Black man is inspiring. He is encouraging. He is determined. He loves his family and wants to see them win. He works hard, pushing himself beyond limits, often carrying burdens that no one sees, all because he wants to provide and protect.

But the Black man has been through so much. From childhood, he was told to be strong, to never cry, and never to show emotion. He is taught that vulnerability is weakness and that expressing his feelings is "acting like a girl." And so, he grows up learning to suppress his emotions, to hide his pain, and to keep his struggles bottled inside. He is told to "man up" no matter what, no matter if he's tired, no matter if he's hurting, no matter if the weight of the world is on his shoulders.

The Black man is expected to endure without complaint. He is rarely given the space to breathe, to say, "I need a break," to ask for rest, to simply exist without the pressure of being everything to everyone. If he takes a moment for himself, he risks being seen as weak. If he expresses his emotions, he fears being judged. So, he stays silent. He carries his burdens alone, moving through life with an invisible armor that protects him but also isolates him.

I feel that the Black man often doesn't know how deeply he is loved. He doesn't always feel like a priority. He doesn't always believe that people truly see him. He is taught not to trust, sometimes from his own experiences, and sometimes from what he has seen growing up. Maybe he has witnessed betrayal. Maybe history has conditioned him to expect disappointment. Maybe he has learned that trusting others, even those closest to him, comes with risk.

But I need the Black man to know this: You are loved. You are seen. You are heard. You are valued. The Black man needs more love, more care, and more concern. He needs more opportunities, more grace, and more understanding. He needs to be reminded that he is not alone, that there are people, Black women, Black men, and people of all races, who truly care about his well-being. Love does not have a color, and there are many who love and uplift the Black man. But no amount of external love will matter until the Black man knows his own worth.

    Once the Black man realizes how significant he is, once he fully embraces his power, his strength, his brilliance, he will be unstoppable. He is already a superhero in the eyes of so many. The moment he truly believes it, he will stand taller, smile brighter, and walk in the confidence that he was born to own.

    That is how I feel about the Black man.

Chapter 1 Summary
I See You:
A Love Letter To The Black Man And Black Woman

In this opening chapter, Dr. Charmaine Marie and Professor Lewis Miles pour out a heartfelt ode to the Black man and Black woman and their strength, their silence, their beauty, and their burdens. They speak as witnesses and believers in their divine design. With tenderness and truth, they acknowledge the emotional truths where vulnerability is punished, and pain must be buried.

Yet despite the weight black men and women carry, often without recognition, they truly see one another. They honor one another beneath the mask. They call each other to remember who they are: loved, valued, seen, and powerful. Because when Black men and women know their worth, really know it, there is no stopping the legacy they can lead.

But loving the Black man and woman didn't start with how they feel about one another; it started with what they were taught about each other. Before the personal revelations came the generational lessons, the family traditions, and the cultural expectations. And

like many, they had to unlearn some things, while holding tight to the truths that still ring eternally.

Chapter 2

Trained to Trust His Strength:

What was I taught to feel about the black man?

Dr. Charmaine Marie

I was taught that the Black man was the foundation of the household. He was the head, the leader, the protector, and the provider. He was the one who made sure nothing and no one threatened his home or his family. He was the man who worked hard to put food on the table, to keep the lights on, to ensure that his family never went without. He was the one who went out into the world, faced its challenges, and carried the weight of responsibility on his back, often without complaint.

The Black man was the fixer. If something in the house broke, he repaired it. If the garage needed work, he handled it. If the furnace went out, he made sure the heat was back on. He locked the doors at night, set the alarms, and ensured that his family slept safely under his watch. He wasn't just maintaining a household; he was maintaining security, stability, and structure.

He was also the spiritual guide. He led his family to church, made sure they had a foundation in faith, and instilled the belief that God was the ultimate provider. He carried the responsibility of ensuring his family not only survived but thrived, physically, emotionally, and spiritually. And yet, despite all he did, there were battles he faced that he couldn't always protect himself from.

I was taught that the Black man had to move carefully in this world. That he had to speak to the police with "yes" and "no" answers, avoid direct eye contact, and remain polite, even when he was disrespected, and even when his dignity was on the line. Because sometimes, even doing everything right wasn't enough to save him.

Still, I was taught to honor him, to build him up, not tear him down, to speak life into him, and not belittle him, to recognize his struggles, and not dismiss them, because everything he did, he did for the good of his family.

The Black man carries an unspoken burden, the expectation to be strong at all times, to provide without fail, to shield his loved ones from the weight of his own struggles. He often fights silent battles, but his love is loud in his actions. That's why I was taught to respect him, uplift him, and never treat him as anything less

than what he is: the backbone of the family, the warrior of the household, and the heart of a love that, when honored and nurtured, can withstand anything.

Trained to Trust Her Strength:
What was I taught to feel about the black woman?

Professor Lewis Miles

I was told to respect her, love her, and stand by her. I was taught to honor and support her, to never lay a hand on her, and to always provide her with protection as her man. These lessons were clear, but understanding the depth of a Black woman's strength, resilience, and needs, has been a journey of its own.

The Black woman is the strongest woman I know. I see her determination to overcome every obstacle placed before her. I witness her achievements, but I also see the struggles she endures while trying to hold everything together: her family, her dreams, and her identity. She wants her Black man to compliment her, to stand beside her, and to understand that even when her time is limited, her love is not. She is on a mission, often fighting battles that go against everything the Black man has been taught to stand for. But instead of resisting her, we, as Black men, must stand with her. We need to find purpose in all that she is doing, not just for herself, but for the greater good of the relationship and our community.

      I believe Black men desire the Black woman more than anything. Yet, our own shortcomings, our fears, our past wounds, and our struggles, too often overshadow the love we seek to build. This lack of healing creates barriers in communication, leaving relationships broken before they can truly flourish. The Black woman is the heart of the Black family, and without her, we risk losing everything. Our children need to see healthy, loving relationships between Black men and Black women. They need to witness respect, partnership, and unity because behavior is learned. The absence of two parents in a household has contributed to the dysfunction we see in many Black men today.

      I feel that we, as Black men, have lost our sense of leadership in our homes. But how can a household survive without its head? We were raised to see our fathers as heroes, the providers, the dependable ones, the authority figures who guide us. So, Black man, where do we measure up in our relationships today?

      How important is it to recognize your Black woman rising, not as competition, but as a partner? To step back into your rightful place, leading with wisdom, strength, and love? Your children need to believe in you.

Your family needs your presence, your guidance, and your leadership.

I believe in Black relationships. I believe in their power, their beauty, and their ability to heal and restore. But we must have real conversations, putting aside egos, past disappointments, and pain. We must learn to forgive, not just for the sake of moving forward, but with the intention of finding real solutions. And in every situation, we must choose to keep it classy, because respect, once lost, is hard to regain.

So, Black man, stop allowing infidelity, anger, and pride to be the downfall of your relationship. Stop seeing your Black woman as an adversary and start working with her. Repair the bridges that have been broken, because if we commit to doing the work, it will work.

Let's sit down, have the hard conversations, and learn to agree to disagree with love and understanding. Know your worth, and recognize that a Black relationship, when honored and respected, is the greatest wealth we can ever have.

Chapter 2 Summary
Trained to Trust Their Strength:
What was I taught to feel about the black man and woman?

In Chapter 2, you explore the powerful information you were taught to believe about the Black man and woman, their strength, leadership, and quiet courage. He was the protector, the provider, the foundation of the home. She was the homemaker, the glue, and the strength. They didn't just do, they endured. They were honored not only for what they accomplished, but for what they bore silently: the systemic pressures, the emotional suppression, and the unspoken expectations to always be strong and selfless.

We speak of a man and woman who shielded their family while rarely being shielded themselves, warriors expected to fight battles with no armor, only pride and purpose. Yet through it all, they were taught to lift one another, speak life into each other, and recognize their roles: he as the head of the household and she as the heart of the household.

This chapter reminds us that respecting a Black man and woman means more than admiration; it means seeing the full weight they carry and still choosing to honor them with intentional love. But what happens when the strength and softness of the Black woman meet the steady resilience of the Black man? What does it look like to love one another beyond survival, to cherish, to protect, and to truly see each other?

As we shift from what we were taught to believe, we move into what we now choose to love. Chapter 3 becomes a celebration of the Black woman and man, through the eyes of a man and a woman who see each other completely, not just for their individual strength, but for her whole soul.

Chapter 3

Loving Her Out Loud:

What do I love about the black woman?

Professor Lewis Miles

What I love about the Black woman is her undeniable strength and unwavering love for what she believes in. She is resilient, determined, and unstoppable. No matter what obstacles come her way, she pushes forward, carrying the weight of the world with grace and power.

I love how the Black woman can manage so much: raising children, building a household, and still making time to chase her dreams. She moves with purpose, turning struggles into triumphs, and always finding a way to create something beautiful out of life's challenges.

I love the way she carries herself, the confidence in her walk, the curves that tell a story of her lineage, and the essence of her aura that is both powerful and alluring. A Black woman's presence commands attention without saying a word. She is elegance, passion, and fire all in one.

Her style is her own, bold and unshaken by trends. She expresses herself fearlessly, knowing that who she is will never go out of fashion. She has risen to heights that inspire generations, breaking barriers and uplifting everyone around her.

I admire her intelligence, her work ethic, and her relentless drive. When a Black woman sets her mind on something, she achieves it, by any means necessary. She is the backbone of families, the nurturer of sons, the protector of daughters, and the unwavering supporter of her man.

The Black woman has endured trials, been mistreated, underestimated, and talked down on. Yet, through it all, she rises, just like the sun in the east, shining brightly for the world to see. She sits high on her throne, a queen in every sense of the word.

I love you, Black woman, for all that you are and all that you will continue to be. You are the heartbeat of the people, the foundation of a legacy, and the epitome of strength and beauty.

Loving Him Out Loud:
What do I love about the black man?

Dr. Charmaine Marie

I love the Black man. I love his heart, especially when it is pure, open, and full of love. I love his strength and the way he carries the weight of the world on his shoulders and still stands tall. I love when a Black man is confident, when he walks into a room knowing exactly who he is, unshaken, unapologetic, and powerful.

I love the way a Black man loves. There is something about the way he gives his heart fully when he's truly in love. I love the way he loves me, the way he sees me, the way he holds me, the way he protects me, not just physically but emotionally. I love how he treats me when he's happy, when he's at peace, and when he feels safe in my love.

I love the way he respects his mother, the way he honors her, acknowledges her, and appreciates her for all she has done. I love the way he loves his children, how he shows up for them, protects them, and provides for them. There's something beautiful about watching a Black man be a father, a mentor, a leader, and a role model, shaping the next generation with wisdom and strength.

I love the way he looks at me, like I'm the most beautiful thing he has ever seen. I love the way he compliments me, how his words lift me up, how he reminds me of my worth. I love the way he talks to me, the way his voice carries assurance, the way he makes me feel secure, just by the way he speaks.

I love his intelligence, his curiosity, his depth. A Black man knows things about history, about family, and about love. He carries wisdom that runs deep, shaped by generations before him, and he shares that wisdom effortlessly. I love his drive, how he commits to his work, how he gets up every morning with purpose, how he shows up and gives his all. And when he comes home, I love that he expects recognition, because he deserves it. A Black man should be praised for his hard work, for his sacrifices, and for the way he provides and protects.

I love watching him when life unfolds just as he planned, when his dreams are coming true, when the effort he put in is finally paying off. I love seeing the fire in his eyes when he's passionate about something, when he believes in something, when he's inspired, and when he's fully locked in on his purpose. There's nothing like witnessing a Black man walk in his greatness.

I love seeing him dressed up in a sharp suit, smelling good, with a fresh haircut and crisp line-up. But I also love him when he's laid-back, comfortable in his own skin, and wearing what makes him feel good. I love a man who isn't afraid to be himself, who can throw on colors that some might say aren't "masculine" and still wear them with confidence. There's something about a Black man in pink, standing tall, unshaken, knowing exactly who he is, knowing he looks good and doesn't need validation from anyone.

I love the Black man. I love everything about him. His essence, his power, his resilience, his softness, his passion, and his drive. And most of all, I love that I get to love him in a way that brings him peace, in a way that makes him feel valued, seen, and understood.

I want him to be the happiest man in the world, and I want to be the reason. I want the love I give and the way I pour into him, to be a reflection of how deeply I cherish him. Because he deserves it. Because he is worthy. Because I love him.

Chapter 3 Summary
Loving Each Other Out Loud

In this chapter, love is spoken loud, proud, and unapologetically. Professor Lewis Miles opens with a poetic tribute to the Black woman, her strength, resilience, elegance, and divine femininity. She is the nurturer, the warrior, the muse. She carries generations in her stride and wears grace like armor. His words are not just admiration; they are reverence.

Dr. Charmaine Marie responds with a kind offering, a soul-deep love letter to the Black man. She uplifts his leadership, his quiet strength, his tenderness, and his need to be seen, heard, and honored. Her praise is intimate, layered with insight, and charged with a desire to love him in a way that restores his peace.

Together, these reflections are a mirror and a balm. They remind us that Black love, at its best, is rooted in deep respect, intentional communication, and shared purpose. It is sacred ground. But love is not always smooth. It is not always poetic.

Sometimes, love speaks truth in a sharp tongue. And if we're going to build something real, we have to confront the hard things too, the missteps, the silence, the resentment, and the pain we've caused one another.

In Chapter 4, we pull back the curtain, no makeup, and no filter, just truth. This is the chapter that risks discomfort in order to spark healing.

Chapter 4

Fixing Us:

Calling Out the Chaos and Calling In the Change

Professor Lewis Miles

I love my people, but I won't ignore the struggles we face, especially the ones we create for ourselves. Too often, I see division where there should be unity, competition where there should be support, and destruction where there should be growth.

One of the things that pains me the most is how often Black men are against each other. Instead of building together, they tear each other down. There's a lack of brotherhood, a lack of support, and, at times, a lack of respect for themselves and the women who stand beside them.

I hate that too many Black men refuse to be great fathers to their children, leaving them to navigate life without the guidance and love they deserve. I hate that so many Black men cross each other out instead of standing together as a force of power, strength, and leadership.

I also feel that successful Black men don't invest in other Black men, not just financially, but in leadership and mentorship. Where are the men pulling the next generation up, showing them the way, teaching them how to break generational cycles? Without strong role models, too many young Black men are left to figure it out on their own, often making choices that lead to destruction instead of success.

It hurts to see Black men neglect their communities, refusing to uplift the places where their families and loved ones live. We should be the protectors and builders of our neighborhoods, not the ones contributing to their downfall. The lack of respect for life, for liberty, and for each other is heartbreaking.

And why is it that Black men struggle to support other Black men in business? Why do we hesitate to invest in each other's success? Instead of being the first in line to uplift, too often, we're the first to tear down. And even more painfully, Black men are often last in education but first in homicide, losing their lives at the hands of one another. That cycle has to stop.

As much as I love the Black woman, there are things that deeply frustrate me. One of the most damaging things I see is Black women keeping their children from their fathers out of spite, using them as weapons instead of allowing them the love and guidance of both parents.

I hate seeing a Black woman walk away from a man who is supporting her and her children, simply because she mistakes his kindness for weakness. Too often, the Black woman is in competition with the Black man instead of uplifting him, standing beside him, and growing with him.

I hate seeing a Black woman who doesn't respect herself or her children, just as I hate seeing a Black man do the same. A woman should hold herself to a high standard, not just for herself, but for the example she sets for the next generation.

And then there's the issue of child support being used as a weapon, forcing a man to pay, knowing the child isn't his, simply out of malice. That kind of bitterness doesn't just hurt the man; it affects the child and the entire family dynamic. I also despise seeing a woman neglect her kids for the attention of a man, prioritizing temporary companionship over her responsibility as a mother.

The Solution: unity and support, but here's what I believe, change is possible. If Black men came together, they could transform each other's lives. If they had the support, mentorship, and investment to achieve more than just survival, to thrive, then they wouldn't feel trapped in circumstances that lead to crime, poverty, and struggle. With opportunities and resources, they could build wealth, strong communities, and better futures for their families.

If Black women truly supported one another, created open conversations, learned from women who had their lives together, and lifted each other up, then better decisions could be made. Poor choices wouldn't have to break families apart. We can't expect better if we aren't taught better.

Across the board, we need to come together, Black men and Black women. We need to open lines of communication, ask questions, share knowledge, and provide real solutions. It starts with accountability. It starts with unity. We don't have to be each other's downfall; we can be each other's greatest strength.

Fixing Us:
Calling Out the Chaos and Calling In the Change

Dr. Charmaine Marie

There are things I love about the Black man, but there are also things that I dislike: things that hurt, confuse, and frustrate me. One of the hardest things to deal with is when he is angry, and I don't even know why. The shift in his mood comes without warning. His words become sharp, his tone disrespectful, and his energy filled with negativity. He walks around with a hardened face, a heaviness in his presence, and a voice that only speaks in complaints.

What's worse is when that anger is directed at me, sometimes for reasons I don't even understand. Maybe I did something wrong, unknowingly, thinking I was doing the right thing. But instead of talking to me, explaining, or helping me see his perspective, he lashes out. And not only does he not tell me how he feels, but he shares how he feels with others, turning what should have been a private conversation into a public embarrassment. I don't find out something is wrong until I hear about it from someone else. That kind of treatment doesn't just hurt, it builds resentment, creates distance, and makes real communication impossible.

Another thing that pains me is hearing some Black men criticize Black women, comparing us to women of other races as if we are somehow less. They say Black women are angry, disrespectful, or hard to deal with, and then turn around and claim that women from other backgrounds will treat them better. But is the problem really related to race? Or is it about the relationship itself, the misunderstandings, the unspoken issues, and the lack of communication? Every relationship, no matter what people are involved, has challenges. So why is it that when a Black woman expresses her frustration, it is held against her in a way that makes her feel like her emotions are a burden rather than a valid response to something that hurt her?

What I truly dislike is the lack of space to express my feelings openly. I don't want to walk on eggshells, afraid that my honesty will lead to an argument, a shutdown, or an emotional explosion. I don't want to silence myself just to keep the peace. A real relationship is built on communication, on saying what needs to be said, listening with an open heart, and finding solutions together. If I must suppress my thoughts, hold back my emotions, or shrink myself just to keep someone happy, then the relationship isn't real.

No one should have to dumb themselves down, filter their truth, or fear being vulnerable with the person they love. Because when that happens, the relationship loses its foundation. Without honesty, there is no trust. Without trust, there is no connection. And without connection, there is no love, only a performance of what love should be.

These are the things I dislike. Not because I want to tear the Black man down, but because I want us to be better. Because I believe in the strength of Black love. And because I know that if we can recognize these issues, confront them, and heal from them, we can build relationships that are strong, fulfilling, and truly unbreakable.

Chapter 4 Summary
Fixing Us: Calling Out the Chaos, Calling In the Change

Chapter 4 is a courageous confrontation, an emotional unmasking of the wounds we've inflicted on each other within the Black community, especially in our most sacred bond: that between Black men and Black women.

Professor Lewis Miles lays out his disappointment, not from a place of bitterness, but from a place of deep love. He expresses his feelings about the absence of brotherhood among Black men, the lack of mentorship, the neglect of fatherhood, and the destruction of community from within. He also holds the Black woman accountable, calling out emotional manipulation, the misuse of child support, and behaviors that undermine family unity. His message: we must choose unity over ego, and purpose over pettiness.

Dr. Charmaine Marie responds in kind, unpacking her pain with poetic clarity. She speaks of emotional unavailability, public disrespect, and the suffocating silence that Black women are often forced to endure. Her words demand emotional maturity, safe spaces for communication, and the right to be heard without punishment. Her message: real love requires honesty, healing, and the courage to have the hard conversations.

Together, this chapter doesn't just vent, it envisions. It's a roadmap for change rooted in accountability, grace, and a deep desire for reconciliation. It's a reckoning, and a revival. But calling out the chaos is only half the healing. The next step? Naming the offense, specifically. Because if we don't name it, we can't change it.

Chapter 5 dives even deeper, not just into general dysfunction, but into the personal offenses we carry. It's not finger-pointing. It's soul-cleansing. It's not blame. It's breakthrough.

This is where we stop dancing around the pain and start digging into it. This is where we name the wounds, what he did, what she said, and what we let happen, because once we name it, we can finally heal it.

Chapter 5

What Hurt Me:

Naming the Pain to Break the Cycle

Professor Lewis Miles

There is a deep disconnect between the Black man and the Black woman, and much of it comes from how we see each other, how we treat each other, and how we've allowed society to shape our relationships. Somewhere along the way, we stopped moving as one.

There was a time when the Black man was the primary provider, and when he succeeded, he made sure to uplift his Black woman alongside him. But today, as more Black women achieve success in their careers, some have distanced themselves from Black men instead of continuing to build with them. Instead of seeing success as something to share, it has, in some cases, created division.

Some Black women have chosen to prioritize independence to the point of rejecting the idea of needing a man at all. In doing so, they have unintentionally offended the Black man, making him feel as though he is no longer valued or necessary.

Instead of working together, it often feels like a battle of who is in control.

Many Black men feel like they are no longer given the respect they once had in relationships. Some Black women now have high expectations for a man, requiring him to meet a certain financial or social status, yet they don't always put in the same effort to support or uplift the kind of man they claim to want.

There's also the painful reality that many Black children are being raised to call another man "Dad," even when their biological father is alive and willing to be in their lives. The Black woman, at times, has spoken negatively about Black men in front of their children, creating a cycle of disrespect that leads to strained father-child relationships.

The Black woman has, in some ways, dismissed the traditional role of the Black man in the household. Some have taken on the mindset that they must be the leader, the alpha, and the sole decision-maker, which makes the Black man feel replaced instead of valued as a partner.

Many Black men feel that the Black woman has become difficult to engage with, not because she is strong, but because she has taken on a role that is more combative than collaborative. Some Black men believe that instead of working together, Black women challenge them at every turn, questioning their leadership and diminishing their role in the home. This tension has created a divide, making it harder for Black men and Black women to come together as a unit. It has led to frustration, miscommunication, and, at times, complete disconnection.

Despite these challenges, there is still hope. The Black man and the Black woman must recognize that they are not enemies, they are partners. The goal should not be to compete, but to uplift one another.

Black women must remember that success does not mean leaving the Black man behind, and Black men must ensure that they are actively stepping up as leaders, providers, and protectors. Both must respect each other's roles and contributions to the family and community. If we can rebuild trust, open communication, and mutual support, we can move forward together instead of apart. The Black man and the Black woman are stronger together, but only if we choose to be.

What Hurt Me:
Naming the Pain to Break the Cycle

Dr. Charmaine Marie

There are certain things that deeply offend me; things that cut to the core of respect, love, and responsibility. Some of these actions are not just personal offenses; they are wounds that weaken the foundation of relationships, families, and the Black community as a whole.

One of the greatest offenses is when a Black man chooses not to take care of his child. When he turns his back and denies responsibility, despite knowing he was part of the creation, it is not just an offense, it is a betrayal. A child should never be left wondering why their father isn't present. Parenthood is not optional, and walking away from that duty is one of the deepest wounds a man can inflict on his own blood.

It is offensive when a Black man raises his hand to a woman, treating her like an opponent instead of a partner. No matter how intense an argument gets, no matter how strong emotions run, resorting to violence is never acceptable. A man should never be so angry that he feels justified in hurting a woman physically, emotionally, or mentally. That kind of anger destroys love. It destroys trust. And it is offensive beyond words.

It is offensive when a Black man calls a Black woman out of her name, especially using words meant to degrade and humiliate her. Calling her a B**** does not make her stronger. It does not make her better. It does not give her power. If a man cannot call her something uplifting like beautiful, intelligent, or powerful, then he should say nothing at all. Words have power, and using them to tear a woman down instead of building her up is nothing short of disrespectful.

Cheating in a committed relationship is another offense that cuts deep. If two people have openly agreed to be together, have built trust, shared dreams, and made a commitment, why is it so easy for some men to break that; to step outside the relationship, entertain other women, and disrespect the very foundation they promised to honor? And it's even more offensive when a man goes as far as having a child outside of the relationship. That level of betrayal is not just painful, it's humiliating.

What's worse is when men wear this behavior like a badge of honor, bragging about their infidelity as if it makes them more of a man. There is nothing manly about breaking a woman's heart or disrespecting the commitment you made.

It is offensive when a man refuses to work, when he expects the woman to carry the financial weight of the household while he sits back, hanging out, playing around, and contributing nothing. Having dreams and passions is important, but until those dreams are producing an income, they are hobbies, not responsibilities. A man's ambition should never come at the expense of his partner's exhaustion. A woman should not be expected to work 40 to 80 hours a week, take care of the home, provide for the children, and still support a man who refuses to step up. A partnership is about balance, and refusing to contribute is not just offensive, it is selfish.

And finally, it is offensive when a Black man refuses to hear a woman's truth. Just because he does not agree does not mean she is wrong. Relationships require communication, understanding, and the willingness to see things from both sides.

When a man dismisses a woman's feelings simply because they are different from his own, he is not just rejecting her perspective, he is rejecting the possibility of growth. True love requires listening. True partnership requires compromise. And when a man refuses to engage in that process, it creates a disconnect that no amount of love can fix.

These are the things that offend me. Not because I want to tear the Black man down, but because I want him to rise. Because I believe in Black love, Black families, and Black unity. And because I know that if we can address these issues, we can create stronger, healthier relationships built on respect, trust, and real, unshakable love.

Chapter 5 Summary
What Hurt Me:
Naming the Pain to Break the Cycle

This chapter is a raw and redemptive unpacking of the offenses that fractured our bond as Black men and women. Professor Lewis Miles and Dr. Charmaine Marie hold nothing back as they expose the silent wounds, unspoken betrayals, and cultural shifts that have pulled us apart.

Professor Miles speaks to the erosion of respect, the way society, success, and shifting gender roles have distorted the sacred partnership between the Black man and woman. He names the pain of being replaced, devalued, and pushed to the margins of the home and family. He pleads for a return to mutual responsibility and shared success, not competition.

Dr. Charmaine Marie counters with her truth: the deep betrayal of fatherlessness, the violence, both verbal and physical, that too many Black women endure, and the emotional labor of trying to love a man who won't listen. Her words are not weapons; they are wounds, reopened with the hope of healing.

Together, they confront infidelity, abandonment, verbal abuse, and broken communication, not to condemn, but to create clarity. Because healing can't happen in the dark. You cannot fix what you refuse to name. This chapter lights the match. Now that the pain has been named, the healing begins.

Chapter 6 asks a simple but transformative question: What can I do to be better? Not they, not them, but me. This chapter shifts the focus inward. It's no longer about pointing fingers, it's about extending hands. It's about building each other back up with love, accountability, and action. Because if we truly want Black love to survive, we have to stop waiting for the other person to change. We must become the change we want to receive.

Chapter 6

Better Together:

Becoming the Partner My Person Deserves

Professor Lewis Miles

The first step in making a better Black woman is to love her fully, not just in words but in actions. I can support her by truly understanding her struggles, putting myself in her shoes, and walking alongside her instead of ahead of her. I can encourage her dreams, celebrate her victories, and be a source of strength when she feels weak.

Respect is key, not just in public but behind closed doors, in every space we share. I can honor her with my words, my actions, and my presence, showing her that she is valued beyond just what she can give. I can be a better father to our children, recognizing the weight she carries and doing my part to lighten her load.

I can pray for her, covering her in love and protection, and when life gets overwhelming, I can hold her close, reminding her that she is never alone. I can be an example, not just to her but to other men, showing them what it truly means to cherish and uplift a Black woman.

I can protect her, not just physically, but emotionally and spiritually, ensuring that she feels safe, seen, and appreciated. I can lead with God's love, guiding her with kindness, patience, and understanding.

And beyond what I do for the woman in my life, I can also take responsibility for the way Black women are treated as a whole. I can speak up, have conversations with other men, and challenge them to do better. Change starts with accountability, and if we, as Black men, commit to standing by our women, respecting them, and honoring their worth, we can create a future where the Black woman is not just strong because she has to be, but because she is supported, loved, and empowered.

Better Together:
Becoming the Partner My Person Deserves
Dr. Charmaine Marie

Loving a Black man means understanding him, his struggles, his dreams, his way of thinking, and the way he moves through this world. It means seeing him for who he truly is and standing beside him in a way that makes him feel supported, valued, and appreciated. So, how can I be a better Black woman for my Black man?

I can start by listening more; really listening. Not just hearing his words, but understanding what's on his mind and how he processes life. I can take the time to see things from his perspective, not just my own, so that instead of always trying to meet in the middle, we can learn to move as one. Compromise doesn't mean giving up my thoughts and feelings, but it does mean being open to his thoughts and feelings, making space for his emotions, and showing him that his thoughts and concerns are just as valid as mine.

I can be more intentional with my words. Every day, I can uplift him with something positive, something affirming. A simple "Good morning, handsome" or "I appreciate you" can shift his whole mood. Words carry power, and I want my words to build him up, not tear him down. I want him to know that he is respected, admired, and cherished, not just in the big moments, but in the everyday ones.

I can also be mindful of how I communicate. The way I ask questions, the way I express my feelings, delivery matters. I never want him to feel like my questions are meant to provoke him or that my words are designed to criticize instead of understand. If he's confused about something, rather than reacting with frustration, I can take the time to clarify, explain, and make sure we are on the same page. Love is about patience, and I can choose to be patient.

Beyond words, I can be intentional about creating peace in his life. I can encourage him to take time for himself, whether it's scheduling a monthly massage, supporting his hobbies, or even planning a weekend where he can just relax and recharge. I want him to feel like he has a safe space with me, a place where he can lay down his burdens, breathe deeply, and be at ease.

But above all, I can be more present. Not just physically, but emotionally and mentally. I can be his friend, his true partner. We can find things to do together that bring us both joy. We can sit down and plan our time together, not in a rigid way, but in a way that ensures we are making the most of each other, making each moment count.

I don't want to assume I know what he needs. I want to listen. I want to learn. I want to love him in the way that fulfills him, not just in the way that I think love should look. That means being vulnerable, being open, and allowing myself to love him in the way that he deserves.

I want my Black man to be satisfied, to be happy, and to be at peace. And I am willing to do the work to make sure that he knows, without a doubt, that he is loved, respected, and deeply valued. Because when we pour into each other, when we truly see and hear each other, when we move as one, we don't just build a relationship, we build something unbreakable.

Chapter 6 Summary
Better Together:
Becoming the Partner My Person Deserves

In this pivotal chapter, Professor Lewis Miles and Dr. Charmaine Marie both take personal responsibility for how they show up in Black love. It's not a blame game; it's a soul check.

Professor Miles lays out a heartfelt blueprint for Black men: love her in action, honor her with your presence, protect her with your words, and cover her in prayer. His message is clear: Black women don't need to carry it all. A better man lightens the load and leads with love, not ego.

Dr. Charmaine Marie responds in kind: she calls herself a higher woman who will listen deeply, communicate clearly, and bring peace into her man's life. She commits to speaking life into him, not just when it's easy, but especially when it's hard. She champions the power of intentional presence, emotional intelligence, and respect that heals.

Together, they declare this truth: Black love thrives when both partners stop waiting to be loved better, and instead become better. But even with love, even with effort, there's one thing that will destroy it all: disrespect. We've seen what happens when words become weapons and love turns into resentment. When people leave and come back expecting the same warmth after bringing the cold.

Chapter 7 digs into the silent killers of Black relationships: unchecked pride, entitlement, and emotional inconsistency. This is where respect is earned, not demanded. This is where apologies come with action, and where legacy begins with how we treat each other when nobody's watching.

Chapter 7

Say Less & Show Up:
Where Love Meets Accountability

Professor Lewis Miles

Black woman, why are you embarrassed by me? Why do you act as if I'm less than, like I'm not worthy of your presence or love? Have you forgotten that I came from you, and that you came from me?

You left me behind, and now you treat me like a mistake, something you wish you never had. But how can anyone else respect me, if the one who's supposed to love me treats me like I'm invisible? We've forgotten how to honor each other. We've forgotten how to protect each other with our words. And in that forgetting, we've damaged our ability to build. But I believe we can change that.

I believe we can restore the foundation of Black love by choosing to speak life into one another daily. Respect isn't just something we demand, it's something we give, even in each other's absence. It's how we speak about each other when no one's watching. It's how we support one another, even when our hearts are hurting. If we learn to truly respect ourselves, then we'll learn how to respect the one we say we love. Because when we see ourselves with value, we'll see that same value in our partners.

Black woman, your words matter. Black man, your tone matters. The way we speak to one another can either build a home, or burn it to the ground. Too many Black relationships end not because of lack of love, but because of a lack of respect. Words filled with bitterness. Actions laced with ego. And the wounds run deep because those words, and those actions, come from someone who once held our heart.

But here's the truth: we've overcome too much together to let our legacy fall apart now. We are powerful apart, but unstoppable together. If we choose healing over hurting, respect over resentment, and love over pride, we can build something worth passing down. We can become the relationship that others look to and say, "That's what I want." Not because it's perfect, but because it's real. Because it's rooted in understanding, forgiveness, honor, and mutual support.

Black love is legacy. And legacy starts with how we treat each other today. Let's be better. Let's do better. Let's show the world what Black love can look like when it's respected, honored, and protected.

Say Less & Show Up:
Where Love Meets Accountability

Dr. Charmaine Marie

Professor Miles, you asked: "Black woman, why are you so embarrassed by me?" Here's my truth: I'm not embarrassed by you, until you embarrass me. It's embarrassing when your actions don't match your words. When you act like you don't love me until I've finally had enough, and then you come back with time, energy, and apologies, only after I'm done. It's embarrassing because the people around us see it. They know it. They say, "He's just using her," and that hurts.

I never thought you were less than me. I never believed you were unworthy of my love or my presence. But when you begin to treat me badly, when disrespect shows up in private and in public, I have to protect myself. I distance myself not because you're unworthy, but because I realize I deserve better than what you're giving me.

You asked how I could forget that we came from each other. I haven't forgotten. I believe that. But love and respect are not about who came from whom. Disrespect is disrespect, no matter what the history is. And once that line is crossed, the relationship shifts. It goes from something good to something difficult to recover.

You said I left you behind. But the truth is, you left first, and not just once. You left emotionally. You left physically. You walked away, thinking there were better options, other women, other homes, and other families. And when those doors closed, you returned, expecting to find me waiting. But you chose to walk away. You chose someone else. You made that decision, and now you're asking why I won't let you come back.

I'm not treating you like a mistake. I'm allowing you to live with the consequences of your choices. You didn't choose me when you had me. And now that the people you chose didn't work out, you want to return to the woman who loved you deeply and gave you everything.

And no, I'm not making you invisible. But when you're not present, when you remove yourself from the life we built, you can't expect to be center stage anymore. You can't walk out and expect the same level of access you once had.

You spoke about honoring one another. Honor doesn't just come when it's convenient. You can't demand respect after you've disrespected me. You can't walk out, hurt me, abandon me, and then return, expecting everything to feel the same. If you want to be honored, you have to stay and do the work. You have to show up. You have to build. You can't keep leaving because of disagreements or distractions. You don't get to walk out, find temporary comfort elsewhere, and expect to come back to the life and love you once had.

Yes, we've forgotten how to protect each other with our words. And when you leave, you say whatever you want. You release every hurtful thing you can think of, assuming you'll never need to come back. But when you do need to come back, you expect those words to vanish, like we forgot. You see, the damage isn't just done in your absence, it's also done in your departure. And the pain of that moment echoes long after you've returned.

I believe in building a home, not burning one down. But I need to build with someone who wants to build with me. And once I realize that you're no longer that person, I'm allowed to move on. I'm allowed to heal. I'm allowed to protect my peace. You say you want to restore Black love, then let's start with consistency. Let's stop having backup plans. Let's stop running to other women when things get complicated. Let's stop praising the grass on the other side until we realize it's not real. I don't want to be your backup plan. I want to be your first choice, and if I'm not, then I choose me.

Black love is powerful, it's legacy. It's the dream. I want the family, the joy, and the wholeness. But I refuse to be disrespected in the process. So yes, let's treat each other with love, from beginning to end, and most importantly, in the in-between, because that's where love is truly proven.

Chapter 7 Summary
Say Less & Show Up:
Where Love Meets Accountability

This chapter is a deep emotional reckoning between the Black man and Black woman, each voicing their pain, their truth, and their unmet expectations. Professor Lewis Miles calls out for respect, recognition, and healing, pleading for the restoration of Black love through honor, communication, and consistency. He laments being dismissed and disrespected by the very woman who once loved him, and urges a return to unity built on accountability and legacy.

Dr. Charmaine Marie responds with unapologetic clarity, explaining that it's not embarrassment she feels, but betrayal. She unpacks the emotional toll of broken promises, inconsistency, and emotional abandonment. She reminds him (and all men) that love without accountability is manipulation, and if respect is expected, it must be earned through action, not just apologies. Her message is firm: legacy requires loyalty, and love without integrity is not love at all.

Together, this chapter serves as a confrontation of generational wounds and a call to higher emotional and relational standards. But what happens when love is present, yet misunderstood? When hearts are willing, but communication falls short? In the next chapter, we move from the fire of confrontation to the fog of misinterpretation, where actions were taken as love, but weren't received as such. This is where we confront one of the most silent killers of Black love: misaligned love languages.

Chapter 8

Too Little, Too Late:

When Effort Comes After Exit

Professor Lewis Miles

Black woman! Do you see how I've loved you? Love isn't just a word I said, it was in everything I did. I didn't just show up for you; I showed up for your children, even though they weren't mine. I invested time, care, and energy, not because I had to, but because my love for you made me want to. But now that we're no longer together, it feels like all that time, all that love, and all those memories, mean nothing to you. It feels like I slept over with the enemy, like all we once shared has been erased by pain, disappointment, and resentment.

Why the distaste for something that once brought us both joy? Why does it feel like, because we didn't work out, now you hate me? I haven't forgotten the love we shared. I haven't erased the memories. Even if we aren't an "item" anymore, I can still appreciate the moments that once meant everything to both of us.

Yes, I hurt you. I cheated. I take full responsibility for that. But let's be honest, by the time I stepped out, we had already started to fall apart. I'd come home and you wouldn't speak. You barely looked at me. I was trying to reach you, trying to talk, but you had already checked out emotionally. I was in the house with you, but I felt alone. And no, it doesn't justify what I did. But it explains why I felt like you wouldn't even notice if I left, or if I gave my attention somewhere else.

I saw the writing on the wall. I knew the end was coming. But even as things were falling apart, I never stopped hoping we could fix it. Then came the part that hurt me deeply, hearing you on the phone with someone else, confiding in another man, sharing our private business. You spoke down about me, exposed my flaws to someone new instead of working through the issues with me. That shattered the little trust I had left.

So here we are, two people who once loved each other deeply, now carrying distrust, miscommunication, and heartbreak. How did we get here? How did Black love change so drastically?

We don't express love the same way, and we never really talked about how we needed to be loved. That's where we went wrong. Black men and Black women often speak different love languages. A Black man might show his love through provision, protection, and presence, being there, fixing things, taking on responsibilities. A Black woman may need affirmation, communication, and emotional intimacy, feeling seen, heard, and appreciated.

When those needs go unmet, we begin to question the love. We grow silent. We grow distant. We start to feel alone, even when we're standing next to each other. And in that silence, we let pride speak for us, and we let fear make our decisions. We hurt each other, not because we stopped loving, but because we didn't know how to love each other anymore.

We failed at translating our love into a language others could understand. But it doesn't have to be the end. Even if we don't end up together, we can learn. We can heal. We can evolve. Black love doesn't have to be bitter. It doesn't have to be rooted in betrayal, resentment, or pride. It can be soft. It can be respectful. It can be profound, healing, and whole. But only if we're willing to understand one another… and meet each other where we are.

Too Little, Too Late:
When Effort Comes After Exit

Dr. Charmaine Marie

Yes, I see how you loved me. I understand that your love wasn't just something you said, it was something you showed. And I appreciated the way you were there not just for me, but for my children. They appreciated you, too. They laughed with you. They enjoyed the moments you gave, and the attention you invested. That mattered. But just because we're no longer together doesn't mean I've erased those memories. It doesn't mean it didn't mean anything. What it means is that the way we move now must look different.

You're welcome to see the children. You can still pour into them. But not in a way that confuses them, or me into thinking we're something we're not. This isn't your home anymore. We're not a couple. And when you come around, it can't feel like you're coming to see me under the guise of seeing the children. I let that happen a few times, and I realized the visit wasn't about the children. It was about you trying to rekindle something that's no longer there.

Yes, we had joyful and beautiful moments. Our relationship had laughter and love, until it didn't. You stepping out, that was the breaking point. Whether we were falling apart or not, cheating isn't a response to silence. It's a betrayal that deepens the silence. If we were disconnecting, what we needed was a conversation, not an escape route. But you stopped coming home. You stopped talking. You started pulling away without a word. And the longer you stayed away, the colder I became.

You say I didn't speak to you when you came back, and that I barely looked at you. But did you ever ask why? Did you ever stop to say, "Let's talk about this distance between us?" No. You wanted closeness, without the conversation. You wanted affection, without accountability.

Yes, I checked out emotionally. Not because I wanted to, but because you made me feel like I was already alone. I waited for you to talk. I waited for you to show up for me the way you showed up for others. But you were too busy rushing out the door. You were always in a hurry, and there was always somewhere else to be.

So, while we felt lonely in the same house, I lived with that loneliness. I didn't seek comfort. I sat in it. And still, I stayed. And no, nothing justifies what you did.

You say you felt like I wouldn't notice if you gave your attention elsewhere. But I did notice. I just stopped fighting for what you clearly didn't want to protect.

You saw the end coming, but you didn't face it with me. Instead, you talked to someone else, gave your energy to someone else, and made your choices with someone else. And then, when I finally tried to open up, to express my hurt, you mistook it for nagging or drama.

And yes, maybe you overheard me on the phone with someone else, confiding in someone who was interested in me. But I wasn't trashing you. I was sharing my experience. I wasn't exposing your flaws. I was trying to rediscover myself. Because by then, you had already left. Maybe not physically yet, but emotionally, you were gone.

You say I shattered your trust. But let's be honest, you were building something new while still living in what was old. You had already moved on. I was still in the relationship, but you had already emotionally and romantically exited.

So no, we don't carry distrust now. We simply live in the reality that this is over. Not because we hate each other. Not because we're bitter. But because the relationship we had no longer exists, and it's not coming back.

You want to know why everything changed so drastically? Because you moved on without a conversation. You made choices based on your new connection without honoring the relationship you were still in. That's where things broke. And love languages? They matter. We never talked about them, but I've since learned mine: Communication. Emotional connection. Consistent appreciation. Not just grand gestures, but simple, honest presence.

I didn't need gifts. I needed you. I didn't need perfection. I needed effort. I needed to know I mattered even when things got hard. But none of that was there. And now it's over, not with bitterness, and not with anger, but with closure.

We'll never be together again, because the foundation is gone. But that doesn't mean I wish you harm. I'm grateful for what we had. I'm even more grateful for what I learned, because I've grown. I've healed. I've evolved. And so have you. And that's what makes this story meaningful.

Our chapter ended, but the lessons from it are now a guidebook for how we move forward, not together, but stronger, wiser, and better prepared to love the right way. So, thank you for the good, for the bad, and for the clarity. Because next time, we'll both love differently, and that's the real blessing in the lesson.

Chapter 8 Summary
Too Little, Too Late:
When Effort Comes After Exit

In Chapter 8, Professor Lewis Miles opens up with vulnerability, expressing his belief that his love was genuine, displayed through presence, provision, and care. But that love, though real, went unrecognized because it was not translated into the emotional language his partner needed. He reflects on how silence and emotional distance crept in long before the betrayal, and while he owns his mistake, he also highlights the pain of being dismissed and misunderstood.

Dr. Charmaine Marie responds with grace and truth. She acknowledges the love he gave but holds firm in her need for emotional presence, communication, and accountability, things that were missing long before the relationship ended. She makes it clear: betrayal isn't a response to disconnect, it's a decision that breaks what little connection remains. Her emotional withdrawal wasn't sudden; it was survival. And while she hasn't erased the memories, she also doesn't romanticize them.

This chapter is an autopsy of love lost in translation. Two people loved, but in different dialects.

By the time they figured out each other's language, the foundation had already crumbled. What remains is not regret, but clarity, a lesson learned in real time, offering both closure and wisdom for future love. But love doesn't just die from lack of effort, it starves in silence. What if the real disconnect wasn't just the way we showed love, but how we listened?

In Chapter 9, we journey from expression to reception, from words spoken to hearts heard. It's called "The Power of Listening: Hearing to Heal, Not to Win", a sacred reminder that healing begins not with being right, but with being present. Because sometimes, the greatest act of love isn't speaking louder, it's listening deeper.

The Journey Back to Real LOVE: A Roadmap for Healing Black Love & Community

Starting with Chapter 9, Dr. Charmaine Marie and Professor Lewis Miles shift from individual reflection to raw truth-telling and emotional release to a place of unity, maturity, mutual understanding, and united restoration. After speaking their truths, venting their pain, and confronting their past, they now meet in agreement, ready to chart a path forward. This next section is not just a dialogue. It's a declaration; a blueprint, a love offering to our people.

Together, they unpack what it truly takes to repair the fractures in our relationships, families, and communities. These chapters serve as one roadmap of many, a heartfelt and hard-earned guide, to help us return to what matters most.

This is the revival of real love: romantic love, Black love, community love, self-love, sacred love, restoration, cultural resurrection, and generational repair. This is the kind of love that holds us together when the world wants to pull us apart. It's about learning to do love well again, because the real revolution is love. Welcome to healing!

Chapter 9

The Power of Listening:

Hearing to Heal, Not to Win

Dr. Charmaine Marie

and Professor Lewis Miles

In many Black relationships, one of the most overlooked acts of love is true listening. We don't mean nodding while preparing your response or waiting for your turn to speak, we mean listening to understand, listening with compassion, and listening without ego.

Too often, communication turns into competition. We hear only to defend, interrupt to correct, or listen with judgment instead of empathy. That's not love. That's self-preservation disguised as connection.

But real love listens with presence. It sits in silence when needed. It offers safety, not solutions. And most importantly, it listens with the intention to care, not to control.

Black love has survived so much, generational trauma, systemic barriers, broken homes, misunderstood emotions, and wounds that go back centuries. One of the ways we begin to repair what's been broken is by simply, yet intentionally, listening to one another.

Listening is:
- Not about fixing. Sometimes your partner doesn't need advice, they need you to just be present and hear their heart.
- Not about agreeing. You don't have to agree to validate someone's experience. You just have to respect it.
- Not about defending yourself. True listening means laying down your ego and picking up empathy.
- A form of love. To listen deeply is to say, "You matter to me. Your voice matters. Your pain matters. You're not alone."

We encourage you to make space to talk without correction and listen without judgment. Put away your phone, your distractions, your assumptions, and lean in, eye to eye and heart to heart. Try asking: "Do you need me to listen, or are you looking for feedback?" This simple question creates boundaries and invites clarity.

We also have to stop weaponizing our partner's vulnerability. When someone opens up, don't use it later to shame or guilt them. Protect it like a sacred gift, because it is.

The truth is that listening is a ministry. Listening is healing, listening is holy, and listening is necessary if we are to raise up the kind of Black love that our children will admire, respect, and want to replicate.

Let's normalize:
- Not interrupting.
- Not assuming we know the full story.
- Not rushing the conversation.
- And not always having something to say back.

Let's normalize holding space, because in that space, relationships grow stronger. And when we create room to really hear each other, we create room to truly love each other.

Chapter 9 Summary
The Power of Listening:
Hearing to Heal, Not to Win

Chapter 9 is a call to sacred attentiveness, a reminder that listening is not a passive act, but an intentional and healing form of love. Dr. Charmaine Marie and Professor Lewis Miles shine a light on one of the most undervalued yet transformative tools in Black relationships: true listening.

Too often, communication becomes a battleground where partners aim to win instead of understanding. Listening is reduced to preparing rebuttals, defending egos, or correcting pain rather than holding space for it. But in its purest form, listening is love, a love that validates without fixing, respects without agreeing, and heals without demanding control.

The authors challenge couples to return to the roots of connection: presence, empathy, and nonjudgment. They call for a shift in how we treat each other's vulnerability, not as ammunition, but as a sacred gift. When we normalize listening with the heart instead of the ego, we don't just communicate, we connect. Because at the core, listening says: "You matter. I see you. I'm with you."

But what happens when we fail to listen, not just to each other, but to the lessons of our past? When we ignore the cries of generations before us, we risk repeating their heartbreak. And far too often, the weight of that unhealed trauma is passed down, wrapped in silence, and inherited through pain.

In Chapter 10, "Breaking Generational Curses in Black Relationships," we confront the patterns we've normalized for far too long. It's not just about healing our love; it's about rewriting the blueprint for the generations watching us because of the real legacy of Black love. It's not just surviving, it's showing our children how to love well.

Chapter 10

Rewriting Our Love Legacy:

Breaking Curses, Building Connection

Professor Lewis Miles & Dr. Charmaine Marie

Can we work together to break the generational curses that have plagued our relationships for far too long? We are reflections of each other. When we tear each other down, our children absorb that pain. They watch, they listen, and they learn, often repeating the same cycles we claim to want to break. Our love, or lack of it, shapes the way they see themselves, their relationships, and their futures.

Our children are growing up with no respect for love or relationships because they have witnessed the breakdown of our love? When our relationship falls apart, our children see it. They heard the arguments. They felt the distance. And when they heard us speak negatively about each other, they internalized that message, learning to see Black love as something broken rather than something sacred.

Children who grow up without their father in the home carry wounds that may never fully heal. If we don't change the way we treat each other, we are teaching our children to expect dysfunction rather than love, and to embrace division rather than unity.

Let's give our children something healthy to see? Let's show them love. Let's show them a partnership. Let's show them what a real man and a real woman who love each other do to show they really love each other.

Chapter 10 Summary
Rewriting Our Love Legacy:
Breaking Curses, Building Connection

In this chapter, Professor Lewis Miles and Dr. Charmaine Marie challenge the deep-rooted patterns of pain that have echoed through generations of Black relationships. They call out the silent teachings passed down through fractured love, absent fathers, and toxic communication.

The truth is clear: our children are watching, and what they witness today shapes how they give and receive love tomorrow. The breakdown of our bonds becomes the blueprint for theirs, unless we choose to rewrite the story. It's a call to action for couples to not only heal individually, but to stand united as living, breathing examples of what real love looks like. It's not just about us, it's about what we pass on. It's about building a future where love is sacred again, and where our children grow up believing in unity, not dysfunction.

But even as we work to break these generational curses, we must be mindful of what we bring into our homes daily. Love is not just what we say; love lives in how we show up.

And that brings us to the next chapter. Sometimes, it's not the arguments that do the most damage, it's the silence. The slammed doors. The cold energy. The emotional distance. Let's talk about the invisible weight that creeps into our homes and affects everyone in them. Let's talk about energy.

Chapter 11

Home Vibes Don't Lie:

The Power of Presence

Professor Lewis Miles and Dr. Charmaine Marie

It happens all the time. You're upset, maybe about work, maybe about finances, or maybe just about life in general. But when you walk through the door, instead of greeting us with love, you bring that frustration inside. You slam doors. You barely speak. You don't smile. You don't even look like you want to be home, and we feel it. The kids feel it.

We're not tearing each other down with words at that moment, but your energy alone is bringing the whole house down. And the truth is, we're counting on you. We want you to be happy. We want to support you. But we can't do that if you won't even let us in.

If you've had a stressful day, I understand. But the first thing you say when you walk in the house shouldn't be filled with frustration. Handle that energy before you step through the door. Take a deep breath in the car. Say a prayer. Listen to some music. Then, when you come inside, show love first, greeting your family with warmth. Hug your children. Kiss me. Let us know that no matter what happened out there, you are happy to be home with us.

And if something is really weighing on you, I want to hear about it. I want you to vent to me, but the reality is, many times, you don't. You hold it in, or worse, you vent to someone else. You laugh with them, talk with them, and confide in them, while your family is left in the dark. And that's not fair. How can you give your laughter, conversation, and energy to outsiders, but come home and give us silence?

Chapter 11 Summary
Home Vibes Don't Lie: The Power of Presence

In Chapter 11, the message is loud without shouting: your energy speaks before your mouth ever opens. This chapter reminds us that love isn't just in what we say, it's in the atmosphere we carry through the front door. Frustration, stress, silence, or coldness may not come with curse words, but they curse the home all the same.

When we come home heavy, without releasing the day's burdens or inviting our family into our emotional world, we rob them of the connection they deserve and need. Our children feel it. Our partners sense it. The house becomes emotionally bankrupt, not because of fights, but because of emotional absence.

This chapter is a charge to check our energy, to greet our homes with intention, warmth, and presence. It challenges Black men and women to stop giving the best of themselves to the outside world, leaving the emotional leftovers for the ones who matter most. Because love isn't just how you act when things are easy, it's how you show up when things are heavy.

Energy isn't the only thing we pass down. Every sigh, every silence, every argument, every act of love, or lack of it, becomes part of our children's inheritance. So, what are we really leaving behind?

In Chapter 12, we go deeper into the wealth that matters most: the emotional, relational, and spiritual legacy we hand off to our children. It's called "The Reality of Generational Wealth", and it's about so much more than money. It's about healing cycles, modeling maturity, and creating a foundation of love, accountability, and peace. Because the next generation deserves more than survival, they deserve a healthy example of what it means to love, lead, and leave a legacy.

Chapter 12

Healing Is the Real Wealth:

Redefining What We Pass Down

Professor Lewis Miles and Dr. Charmaine Marie

Generational wealth is more than financial success, it's about the love, respect, and values we pass down. And if we're being honest, we have a lot of soul-searching to do. We must take a deep look at ourselves, acknowledge what we could have done better, and commit to being better for the sake of our children and future generations.

We can't undo the past, but we can be honest about our mistakes. We can own what went wrong, explain how we've learned from it, and show our children a different path moving forward. Because if we truly want them to grow up strong; mentally, emotionally, and spiritually, we must first heal ourselves. That means taking the time to self-reflect, seeking help if necessary, and doing the internal work to break toxic cycles.

Too often, we focus on blaming each other, rather than asking ourselves, what could I have done differently? But healing isn't about pointing fingers, it's about accountability. If we don't change how we treat one another, we're teaching our children to expect dysfunction instead of love, to embrace division rather than unity.

Our kids don't just hear our words, they feel our energy. They see how we interact, how we handle conflict, and how we either build each other up or tear each other down. A son who watches his father disrespect his mother internalizes that message, whether he agrees with it or not. And one day, he may repeat that same behavior, not because someone told him to, but because it's what he was shown. The same goes for our daughters. They learn how to treat men, how to set boundaries, and what to accept based on the example we set.

So, instead of passing down pain, let's pass down healing. Instead of normalizing brokenness, let's normalize love and respect, even when relationships don't work out. We don't have to be enemies. We don't have to be bitter. We don't have to let past wounds dictate our future.

True happiness means letting go of resentment. It means handling co-parenting with grace, exchanging our children with a smile, and creating a peaceful environment for them to thrive in. If we claim to be happy, then our actions should reflect that happiness. If we've moved on, then there should be no lingering hostility.

At the end of the day, the way we treat each other today shapes the Black family of tomorrow. And the Black family deserves to be strong, united, and thriving. We don't have to accept the negative narratives that have been placed on us. We do measure up. We are capable of love, unity, and success, both in our homes and in our communities. But it starts with us. It starts with healing, accountability, and a decision to break the cycle. So, let's move forward with love, maturity, and understanding. Let's do better for each other, for our children, and for the future, because they're watching, and they deserve better.

Chapter 12 Summary
Healing Is the Real Wealth:
Redefining What We Pass Down

In Chapter 12, the lens of wealth is recalibrated, shifting from dollars to deep internal healing. It argues that true generational wealth isn't just about passing down assets, but passing down wholeness: emotional intelligence, spiritual grounding, respect, and accountability.

This chapter forces us to look in the mirror and ask the hard questions: What cycles are we continuing? What wounds are we handing down wrapped as inheritance? And most importantly, what are we teaching our children, not just with our words, but with our actions, our conflict, and our love (or lack of it)?

Healing, we're reminded, is a decision. One that requires grace, maturity, and a real willingness to do the work. Because how we love today becomes how they love tomorrow. So, if we truly want our children to thrive, we must give them more than survival, we must give them an example worth imitating. Because while we're fighting to fix what's happening inside our homes, we're also battling what's being said about us outside of them.

That brings us to Chapter 13. How much of our pain is personal, and how much has been programmed? How much of our disconnection is internal, and how much has been carefully orchestrated through music, media, and manipulation?

In Chapter 13: Resurrecting Black Love: What Society Tried to Bury, We're Reviving, we go to war with the narratives that were never ours to begin with. It's time to pull the mask off the lie that says Black men can't love. To tear down the myth that Black women are hard to love. It's time to rewrite the script and take back the sacredness of Black love, because when Black love is restored, everything around it begins to rise.

Chapter 13

Resurrecting Black Love:

What Society Tried to Bury, We're Reviving

Professor Lewis Miles and Dr. Charmaine Marie

Was Tupac right when he said, "We'll have a race of babies that will hate the ladies?" Because if we're being honest, look around. We're seeing too many broken bonds, too many babies being raised without the foundation of respect and love between the two people who brought them into the world. And it begs the question, how did we get here? Is what we hear in music, Is what we see on social media, Is what we're shown in movies and online clips, really who we are? Or is it just who we've been told we have to be?

Black woman, why do you allow a man to call you a B**** or an H** when you were raised to be a queen? You were taught to carry yourself with pride, to honor your body, your mind, and your spirit. So why do you now accept less than what you were born to deserve?

Black man, why do you accept the lie that tells you your Black woman is your enemy? You were raised by a Black mother. You may have daughters who look up to you. So why let this world convince you that your love for your own reflection is weakness? When did we stop believing in each other?

Media tells us that Black men are aggressive, absent, and untrustworthy. Media tells us Black women are loud, bitter, and hard to love. And we've let that seep into our relationships, into our homes, and into our hearts. We've accepted dysfunction as culture. We've normalized disrespect as personality. We've mistaken pain for passion. But we're more than the broken narratives. We're more than memes and music videos. We are strength! We are beauty! We are legacy!

Black woman, will you stop believing what the world says about your Black man? He is not a menace. He is not disposable. He's a man trying to navigate a world that told him he would never survive in it. Doesn't he deserve someone to believe in him? To care for him? To love him enough to help him become the man he was created to be?

Black man, will you stop punishing your Black woman for being strong in a world that demanded she had to be? She's not your enemy. She's not trying to replace you. She's tired of holding it all together on her own. She needs your presence, your partnership, and your protection.

So, the real question is: How do we change this status quo? How do we rebuild trust, respect, and commitment in our relationships and in our communities? It starts with intention. It starts with unlearning everything this world told us about each other. It starts with choosing to see each other's humanity before we see the stereotypes.

We need to love like we're healing generations. Because we are. We need to respect like we're teaching our children how to love. Because we are. We need to protect each other like our future depends on it. Because it does. When Black love is restored, Black families thrive. When Black families thrive, Black communities heal. And when our communities heal, our legacy rises.

Chapter 13 Summary
Resurrecting Black Love:
What Society Tried to Bury, We're Reviving

Chapter 13 is a bold call to arms and a spiritual revival for Black love. It tears down the toxic lies society has planted in our minds and hearts, lies that pit Black men and women against each other, and portray our love as dysfunctional, disposable, or doomed. This chapter challenges us to unlearn the stereotypes, question the narratives, and reclaim the truth: Black love is powerful, sacred, and revolutionary.

We are not the broken images we see in media. We are kings and queens, builders of legacy, and keepers of divine connection. But in order to resurrect what society tried to bury, we must see one another with fresh eyes. We must stop punishing each other for wounds the world gave us and start choosing intentional, healing love. Because when we repair the foundation between us, we don't just restore relationships, we rebuild families, and we resurrect our communities.

But truth alone isn't enough. It's not just about rejecting the world's lies, it's about learning to speak each other's truth with gentleness, grace, and courage.

If we are going to restore Black love, we must go deeper. We must create space for emotional intimacy, for real communication, and for the kind of support that doesn't just feel good, it heals. Because beneath the armor, we're all still carrying something.

In Chapter 14, we explore what it truly means to build safe spaces inside our relationships, where our Black men can finally breathe, where our Black women can finally rest, and where love isn't just spoken, it's lived.

Chapter 14

Emotional Wealth:

The Love That Protects and Provides

Professor Lewis Miles and Dr. Charmaine Marie

In general, many men, especially Black men, have been taught to carry the weight of the world on their shoulders. When they're struggling, and even when they need help, they often remain silent. They push through pain, suppress emotion, and try to figure things out alone. Not because they don't want support, but because somewhere along the way, they were taught that needing support is weakness.

So instead of leaning on their partner, many Black men become self-reliant to a fault. They try to solve everything in silence, thinking that's the "strong" thing to do. But silence doesn't heal. It isolates, and isolation leads to emotional breakdown. It's more than just pride, it's also a trust issue.

Many Black men struggle to open up because they're unsure if they'll be safe in their vulnerability. They're uncertain if the person they confide in will hold their truth with grace, or throw it back in their face during hard times. So instead, they choose silence, hoping it'll protect them from disappointment.

Genuine relationships, lasting, deep, transformational relationships, aren't built on silence. They're built on partnership. It's not just about financial contribution. It's not just about traditional roles. It's about being present, voluntarily, intentionally, and emotionally. It's about being willing to give of yourself, not just your resources, but your heart, your words, and your transparency. That's the kind of connection that creates appreciation. That's the kind of relationship that teaches understanding, that nurtures grace, and that strengthens the bond between a Black man and a Black woman.

So, Black woman, how can you help? By becoming a safe place for emotional honesty.
By not using a man's vulnerability as a weapon during moments of frustration or conflict. By not comparing him to others, or tearing him down when he's already trying to stand tall on broken ground. Encourage him. Inspire him. Speak to the king in him, even when life tries to convince him he's nothing more than a failure. Be open. Be present. Do the inner work for yourself too, so that you can help your man become the best version

of himself, not just for you, but for himself. Stand firm and love your man to his core. Love him to the place where he begins to heal. Love him in a way that builds him, not breaks him.

And Black man, a woman needs all of that from you, too. We don't need relationships that are simply roles and routines. We need relationships that are built on emotional truth, intentional love, and mutual respect, because real Black love isn't built on perfection. It's built on partnership. It's built on grace. It's built on two people who are willing to take their armor off, even after the world has tried to make them wear it all day. If we can create these safe spaces for each other, we won't just love longer, we'll love better.

Chapter 14 Summary
Emotional Wealth:
The Love That Protects and Provides

In this chapter, we unpack the emotional currency of Black love, where safety, vulnerability, and spiritual protection are more valuable than silver and gold. We confront the silent weight Black men often carry, the silence they were taught was strength, and the isolation that silence creates. But real strength lies in connection, in building partnerships where both people feel seen, heard, and safe to lay their burdens down.

Emotional intimacy isn't just about soft moments and sweet words, it's about trust, consistency, and intentional presence. We explore how Black women can become a refuge, not a battlefield, and how Black men must show up emotionally, not just financially. When both partners remove their armor and choose grace over ego, they build a love that doesn't just survive, it transforms. Emotional safety isn't just a luxury. In Black love, it's the lifeline.

But love without provision is only half the equation. Emotional safety is vital, yes, but so is financial stability. Our people have survived too much and sacrificed too long to keep circling cycles of lack.

So, what is the next step in fortifying Black relationships? Building a partnership that protects not only hearts but homes. If emotional wealth is the soul of Black love, financial wealth is the spine. Let's talk about money, mindset, and the mission to leave more than memories behind. Let's talk about building Black legacy.

Chapter 15

Secure the Bond and the Bag:

Black Love Meets Financial Power

Professor Lewis Miles and Dr. Charmaine Marie

Building financial stability within Black relationships requires a collaborative approach, emphasizing trust, effective communication, and shared goals. Addressing economic challenges together can strengthen the partnership and lay the foundation for long-term success.

Engaging in lawful, consistent employment is crucial for personal integrity, financial stability, and the well-being of one's family. Relying on illegal activities, such as selling stolen goods or illicit substances, not only jeopardizes your freedom but also undermines the foundation of trust and security within your household. Even if it means starting with an entry-level position at a fast-food restaurant, every form of honest work contributes positively to your family's future.

Having a criminal record is a challenge, but it shouldn't be a barrier to employment. Many employers are open to hiring individuals with past convictions, recognizing the value they bring to the workforce.

Resources are available to assist in this process, such as the Equal Employment Opportunity Commission's guidance on arrest and conviction records. Additionally, some states have implemented "Ban the Box" policies to encourage fair hiring practices. It's essential to be proactive, seek out these opportunities, and demonstrate your commitment to making positive changes.

Concerns about low wages or child support deductions shouldn't deter you from seeking employment. Any income is better than none, and fulfilling child support obligations is both a legal duty and a moral commitment to your children's well-being. If you're experiencing financial hardship, you can request a review of your child support order to better reflect your current situation.

Aspiring to own your own business is commendable, but it's essential to have a stable income during the planning and development stages. Working a steady job not only provides financial support but also teaches valuable skills and work ethics that are essential for entrepreneurship. Remember, a dream without a plan and action remains just a dream.

In relationships, both partners should contribute to the household, whether financially or through other means. Relying solely on one partner's income can create strain and imbalance. By both individuals working and supporting each other, you build a partnership based on mutual respect, shared responsibilities, and common goals. This collaborative effort strengthens the relationship and sets a positive example for any children involved.

In essence, embracing honest work, regardless of the position, and actively contributing to your family's needs fosters a sense of purpose, responsibility, and dignity. It's not just about earning a paycheck; it's about building a legacy of integrity and resilience for yourself and future generations.

In many relationships, one partner may naturally assume a more active role in managing finances due to their expertise or interest. While this can be practical, it's essential that both partners remain engaged in financial decisions. This collaborative approach ensures transparency, fosters mutual trust, and prevents misunderstandings. Regular discussions about budgeting, saving, and spending can help both individuals feel empowered and informed. As highlighted by financial experts, open communication about money matters is crucial to prevent financial infidelity and build a strong foundation.

Financial disparities can create tension in relationships, especially if one partner feels unsupported during times of financial hardship. It's important to challenge stereotypes, such as the notion that Black women are less likely to support a partner facing financial difficulties. In reality, many Black women have demonstrated resilience and commitment by supporting their partners through various challenges, including financial setbacks and co-parenting responsibilities. Recognizing and valuing this support is vital for relationship harmony.

Clear and compassionate communication is the cornerstone of navigating financial challenges. Addressing economic issues proactively, rather than waiting for problems to escalate, can prevent misunderstandings and resentment. Approaching these conversations with empathy and without assigning blame encourages a problem-solving mindset. As noted in discussions about financial dynamics in relationships, understanding each other's perspectives and working collaboratively leads to more positive outcomes.

Creating a joint financial plan that reflects both partners' values and aspirations can enhance unity and direction. This plan should encompass budgeting, saving for future goals, and strategies for debt management. Regularly revisiting and adjusting the plan ensures it remains aligned with evolving circumstances and objectives. By working together towards common financial goals, couples can strengthen their bond and build a secure future.

Fostering financial stability in Black relationships involves mutual respect, open communication, and shared responsibility. By challenging stereotypes, maintaining transparency, and collaboratively planning for the future, couples can navigate financial challenges effectively and build a resilient partnership.

Chapter 15 Summary
Secure the Bond and the Bag:
Black Love Meets Financial Power

In this chapter, we shift from emotional intimacy to economic integrity, because love doesn't thrive in lack. We speak to the power of building together: not just feelings, but futures. Black relationships flourish when both partners are committed not only to each other but to creating a stable financial legacy rooted in honesty, discipline, and shared vision.

We name the elephant in the room: illegal hustles, past records, financial imbalances, and societal systems that make stability harder to achieve, and harder to talk about. But through truth, trust, and teamwork, couples can create wealth that doesn't just support a lifestyle, but sustains a legacy.

Financial contribution is not just about the paycheck, it's about presence, accountability, and purpose. When partners communicate transparently, respect each other's efforts, and align their money mindset, they turn survival into strategy. From child support and employment barriers to entrepreneurship and shared budgeting, this chapter is a call to action for couples to become economic allies in the fight for generational wealth.

Money is not the only thing we need, in order to build something lasting. Wealth gives us resources, but faith gives us roots. In the storms of life, even the most financially stable relationship can lose its footing without a deeper foundation. So where do we turn when love is tested, when emotions run dry, and when plans fall apart? We turn upward. We turn inward. We turn to faith.

In the next chapter, we explore how Black love becomes unbreakable when it's grounded not just in logic or lust, but in divine alignment. Because when God is at the center, the relationship doesn't just survive, it transcends.

Chapter 16

Anchored in the Almighty:

The Spiritual Backbone of Black Love

Professor Lewis Miles and Dr. Charmaine Marie

Integrating spirituality into Black relationships is a foundational pillar, fostering a more profound understanding, mutual respect, and resilience. By placing God at the center of their union, couples can navigate life's challenges with a shared sense of purpose and divine guidance.

Historically, spirituality has been a cornerstone in the Black community, offering strength and solace during trying times. For couples, this spiritual foundation can translate into a relationship grounded in shared values and unwavering support. Engaging in joint spiritual practices, such as prayer and scriptural study, not only deepens emotional intimacy, it also aligns partners with principles that promote love, patience, and understanding.

Praying together is a profound act that fosters vulnerability and trust. It allows couples to openly share their hopes, fears, and gratitude, reinforcing their connection. This practice invites divine presence into the relationship, creating a sacred space where both partners can find comfort and guidance. Couples who regularly pray together often experience enhanced intimacy, and are better equipped to work through difficult issues.

A relationship anchored in spirituality equips couples with tools to handle adversity with grace. Faith instills values of forgiveness, empathy, and unconditional love, which are essential components for enduring partnerships. By seeking guidance from spiritual teachings and mentors, couples can address conflicts constructively, ensuring their relationship remains rooted in mutual respect and understanding.

Being part of a faith-based community offers couples additional layers of support and accountability. Engaging with like-minded individuals who uphold similar values provides encouragement and practical advice, reinforcing the couple's commitment to their shared spiritual journey. These communities can serve as pillars of strength, offering resources and guidance that promote relational and spiritual growth.

In essence, intertwining spirituality with Black love not only fortifies the bond between partners but also establishes a legacy of faith and resilience. By

keeping God at the center, couples create a partnership that thrives on divine guidance, mutual respect, and enduring love.

Chapter 16 Summary
Anchored in the Almighty:
The Spiritual Backbone of Black Love

In this chapter, we explore the sacred intersection of spirituality and Black love. We affirm that when couples place God at the center of their union, their relationship is built on more than affection, it is built on divine purpose.

Through prayer, shared faith practices, and alignment with spiritual values, couples develop tools for emotional intimacy, forgiveness, and resilience. The spiritual foundation doesn't just sustain the couple, it uplifts them, guiding them through trials with grace and reinforcing their bond with unwavering love and shared legacy. Faith isn't just a private practice; it becomes a partnership principle.

As couples ground themselves spiritually, the next step is to express that faith outwardly, through action, service, and shared purpose. When love is lived out loud, it becomes a force in the world. That's where we turn now: to love that moves, love that builds, and love that shows up beyond just the relationship.

Chapter 17

Love in Action:

Strengthening the Bond Through Shared Purpose

Professor Lewis Miles and Dr. Charmaine Marie

Engaging in meaningful activities beyond the confines of a romantic relationship can significantly strengthen the bond between partners. Participating together in community service, such as feeding programs and charity work, or engaging in joint physical activities like exercising, fosters teamwork and mutual support. These shared experiences not only build trust and respect but also provide opportunities for partners to witness and appreciate each other's dedication and values.

For Black men, involvement in such collaborative endeavors can serve as a source of motivation and engagement within the relationship. Actively supporting and participating in their partner's interests and initiatives demonstrates commitment and reinforces the partnership. This mutual investment helps in cultivating a deeper connection, especially for individuals who may not have previously experienced healthy relational dynamics.

By setting and achieving small goals together, couples lay the foundation for a resilient and respectful relationship. These joint accomplishments, whether through community involvement or shared personal projects, enhance understanding and cooperation. They create a shared narrative of success and collaboration, which are essential elements for a thriving partnership.

In essence, stepping outside the traditional boundaries of a relationship to engage in collective activities enriches the partnership. It fosters personal growth, strengthens emotional bonds, and builds a legacy of mutual support and shared purpose.

Chapter 17 Summary
Love in Action:
Strengthening the Bond Through Shared Purpose

In this chapter, we explore how love deepens when it moves beyond private affection into public, purposeful action. Whether it's serving in the community, supporting each other's dreams, or setting and reaching shared goals, couples that build together grow stronger together.

For Black men especially, engaging in joint efforts creates not just momentum, but motivation, purpose, and belonging. These shared experiences reinforce commitment, inspire mutual respect, and forge deeper emotional connections. This is what happens when love stops sitting still and starts showing up in the world.

But real love doesn't stop at what we do for each other. It echoes into how we lead the next generation. When Black love is lived out with purpose, power, and presence, it teaches, it transforms, and it leaves a legacy. That legacy begins at home.

Chapter 18

Bloodline & Bond:

Teaching Our Children What Real Love Looks Like

Professor Lewis Miles and Dr. Charmaine Marie

If we want to raise up a generation of strong, healthy Black relationships, we must first be willing to be open, honest, and real, with ourselves and with each other. It can't just be the blame game: blaming the Black man or blaming the Black woman. It's going to take both of us, and God at the center, to rebuild the kind of love we want our children to grow up believing in.

The truth is, a happy wife helps make a happy home, but so does a happy man. Both matter! And when both are in alignment, the home flourishes. Our children need to see us praying together, leading with love, and seeking God first as a family. When kids see that, it sticks. It sets a standard. It shows them how a home is supposed to feel: safe, spiritual, and strong. And when we say "healthy Black love," we don't mean perfect. We mean honest. We mean accountable. We mean real. We mean respectful, even in separation.

The truth is, even if the relationship ends, the love, the peace, and the maturity shouldn't. Children should never witness hate between two people who once shared love. Even after a breakup, respect should remain.

We can't keep sweeping these conversations under the rug. We have to talk about it. We have to face it. We have to heal it. For me, Black love, real Black love, is one of the greatest relationships known to mankind. And when that love is rooted in God, guided by purpose, and led with truth, it becomes unstoppable. It becomes legacy.

I've never walked away from a relationship where I didn't still want the best for the person. Even if my actions were misunderstood or my words didn't always land right, my heart has always leaned toward forgiveness, not hate. I'd rather forgive than hold bitterness. That's the kind of energy we need more of. That's the example we need to set for the generation coming behind us.

We as a people have to stop hating one another. Stop tearing each other down. Start being proud of one another and supporting what's commendable. When one of us wins, we all win, and that includes in our relationships.

We're quick to judge, but slow to celebrate and support. And too often in Black love, we give up before we give it a real chance. Yes, infidelity hurts. Yes, betrayal is real. But those things don't always mean a relationship can't be saved. Some of the greatest relationships have grown through trials. No love worth having ever comes without a testimony. This book, "Let Love Lead: Reclaiming The Power of Black Love", is not about blame. It's about healing, hope, and honesty. It's about shifting the statistics on failed Black relationships, and giving us something to fight for and believe in again.

And part of that is knowing: If I'm sick, will you still be there? If I'm broke, can I count on you? If things fall apart, will you fight with me or walk away from me? If you're a man who leaves the moment things get hard, ask yourself: What kind of example are you leaving behind? And if you're a woman who only stays when the money is flowing, ask yourself: Was the love ever real?

Let's teach our sons that real men stay. Real men lead. Real men love one woman, and love her well. Let's teach our daughters that a Black woman is worthy of love, loyalty, and leadership. Let's show them that commitment doesn't mean pain; it means partnership.

And let's stop thinking that being with multiple people makes us powerful. Real power is in choosing one person and building something that lasts. That's what makes love legendary.

Let's raise a new standard. Let's teach our children how to love. Let's lead by example. Let's show the world that Black love is not broken, it's beautiful, it's bold, it's still here, and it starts with us.

Chapter 18 Summary
Bloodline & Bond:
Teaching Our Children What Real Love Looks Like

This chapter calls us to accountability, not just for ourselves, but for the generation coming behind us. It's a bold reminder that the way we love, shapes what our children will come to believe about relationships, family, and faith. By modeling healthy Black love, grounded in honesty, mutual respect, and spiritual alignment, we lay the foundation for homes that heal, not harm.

We challenge the blame game, we reject bitterness, and we replace those patterns with compassion, maturity, and a commitment to rebuild. Whether relationships last or evolve, we must protect the integrity of love for our children's sake. Because Black love, when rooted in God and purpose, is not just beautiful, it's revolutionary, and its legacy starts at home.

Before we can build that legacy for others, we must first do the work within. The healing starts in our own hearts, in our own minds, and in our own prayers.

Before we teach our children how to love, we must reflect on how we love. That reflection begins now.

Chapter 19
Rebuilding Us:
The Final Mirror

Professor Lewis Miles and Dr. Charmaine Marie

Before we close this book, take a sacred pause. This is not just a chapter. This is a mirror. Not the kind that shows your face, but the kind that shows your soul. Find stillness. Turn off the noise. Silence your defenses. Let your heart breathe.

You've heard the voices. You've read the truths. You've walked through the ache, the joy, the confrontation, and the clarity. But now, the question is: What will you do with it? This final reflection is for you. Not for your partner, your past, or your pain, but for your becoming.

Take these fourteen questions into the quiet with you:

1. What have I truly learned about myself through this journey?
2. What patterns do I see in my own actions, expectations, or emotional walls?
3. Am I loving the way I want to be loved? Or am I repeating what hurt me?
4. Who or what do I still need to forgive?

5. Am I holding onto wounds that now hold onto me?

6. What would freedom feel like if I finally released the pain, the blame, and the betrayal, even if I never get an apology?

7. How can I help heal Black love in my community?

8. Am I speaking life into, or only talking about its failures?

9. Am I being the example of what's possible, or just echoing the past?

10. Whether I'm single, partnered, or healing, am I contributing to the solution?

11. Where is God in my relationships?

12. Do I invite Him in when I'm choosing love, or only when love breaks down?

13. What would shift if I let God lead the way I lead my heart?

14. What's one thing I can do today to love better, stronger, and wiser? Is it listening more? Trusting more? Speaking life? Setting boundaries?

Whatever it is, do it today. One action. One shift. One seed of love.

The Mirror, is Now Facing Forward. This book doesn't end here, it begins again every time someone decides to love more deeply, more intentionally, and more truthfully. You are not just the reader. You are the ripple. If you want to "Let Love Lead", start with you. And as you heal, restore, and rise, so does the future of Black love.

About the Authors

Professor Lewis Lee Miles Sr. is a visionary author, resilient father, and aspiring humanitarian whose life story is one of hard-earned wisdom, transformation, and unshakable hope. Though currently incarcerated at a federal correctional facility in Forrest City, Arkansas, Professor Miles is far from forgotten, and even further from defeated.

At 54 years old, he is actively working to rewrite the narrative of his life. Once tangled in the cycles of hardship, loss, and misrepresentation within the justice system, he now uses his voice, mind, and faith to uplift others and create a legacy of positive impact. His purpose and vision reach far beyond prison walls.

Born into humble beginnings, Professor Miles endured tragedy that would have broken many. After losing his wife and facing immense financial hardship, he turned to decisions that ultimately led to his incarceration. In 2018, he was offered a 4-year plea deal, but due to misinformation, misrepresentation, and what he believes to be a clear violation of his constitutional rights, he ended up receiving a sentence grossly disproportionate to his role in the case. Throughout the legal process, the same attorney and prosecutor represented all phases of his case, leaving him vulnerable to manipulation, with no change of counsel or proper support during critical moments.

Professor Miles' post-trial life brought even deeper grief, losing both his mother and father within a short time frame, all while navigating a failing appeal system that overlooked the obvious injustices in his case. Despite these trials, he made a vow: to rise again, not just for himself, but for the many men and women who feel forgotten, voiceless, and misunderstood behind bars.

Partnering with his dear sister and friend, Dr. Charmaine Marie, Professor Miles co-authored a powerful and purpose-driven book while incarcerated, one that speaks to redemption, responsibility, and the real meaning of love, family, and change. Through this work, he hopes to be a light for others who may feel trapped by past choices and/or overlooked by society. Their collaboration is a testimony to the power of belief, partnership, and possibility.

Professor Miles is also laying the foundation for a new chapter, one that includes writing more books, and developing streams of passive income. His mission is to mentor young people, support returning citizens, and be a living testament to what it means to fall, learn, rise, and lead with compassion.

Professor Lewis Lee Miles invites readers and supporters to walk this journey with him, not just through the pages of his work, but through advocacy, prayer, and hope for a second chance. His story is not one of shame, but of strength. It is not just about time served, it's about purpose discovered.

Dr. Charmaine Marie, Ed.D., is a devoted advocate for youth, blending her love for writing with a profound passion for empowering young minds. As a diverse author, Dr. Charmaine Marie crafts books designed to inspire and uplift, providing young readers with the tools to build a solid foundation in life, self-love, and greatness. Her writing is a reflection of her unwavering commitment to nurturing the potential within each young person, guiding them toward a future marked by success and fulfillment.

While she wears many hats: Realtor®, Executive Director of Real L.O.V.E., US Navy Veteran, and Founder and Owner of Real LOVE Executive Luxury Wine. Dr. Charmaine Marie's first love is the youth and their outcomes in life. She pours her heart into creating works that resonate with young readers, encouraging them to embrace their unique strengths and pursue their dreams with confidence. Through her books, Dr. Charmaine Marie hopes to leave a lasting, positive imprint on the next generation, helping them navigate their journey with resilience, self-respect, and a sense of purpose.

We really appreciate you taking the time to read,

Let Love Lead

Reclaiming the Power of Black Love

Please do a review on Amazon.com

to let us know what you think.

www.ingramcontent.com/pod-product-compliance
Lightning Source LLC
Chambersburg PA
CBHW070503100426
42743CB00010B/1746